UNLOCKING INNOVATION FOR DEVELOPMENT

ACTION UPDATE: WHAT WORKED AND WHAT DIDN'T FOR ADB'S FIRST INNOVATION REGIONAL TECHNICAL ASSISTANCE PROJECT

FEBRUARY 2020

ASIAN DEVELOPMENT BANK

ADB

CONTENTS

TABLES, FIGURES, AND BOX

ACKNOWLEDGMENTS

Technical assistance administrators: Susann Roth, Mary Jane Carangal-San Jose, Josephine Aquino, Dennis Von Custodio

The following provided invaluable input in the preparation of the report: Raquel Borres, Sharyn Bow, Claudia Buentjen, David Freedman, Hiddo Huitzing, Yukiko Ito, Ki Joon Kim, Rouselle Lavado, Shruti Mehta, Chris Morris, Minh Nguyen, Kirthi Ramesh, Karin Schelzig, Lu Shen, Lotte Schou-Zibell, Daniela Schmidt, Elaine Thomas

Writer and production manager: Jane Parry
Copy editor: Wickie Mercado
Proofreader: Karen Williams
Layout design: Keisuke Taketani

ABBREVIATIONS

4Ps	Pantawid Pamilyang Pilipino Program
ADB	Asian Development Bank
BAPPEDA	Badan Perencana Pembangunan Daerah/District Planning and Development Office, Indonesia
DMC	developing member country
ICT	information and communication technology
iRAP	International Road Assessment Programme
Kinerja	Local Governance Service Improvement Program, Indonesia
PEA	Provincial Electricity Authority, Thailand
SaaS	Software as a Service
SDG	Sustainable Development Goal
TA	technical assistance
TBC	Toilet Board Coalition
WHO	World Health Organization

INTRODUCTION

INNOVATION IS IMPERATIVE FOR DEVELOPMENT

Research has shown that innovation can serve as a driver of growth at many levels, from businesses to countries and as a catalyst for regional development.[1]

Developing countries need new ways to create value because they can no longer rely on exploitation of natural resources to maintain the current pace of growth. They must find new and faster ways to develop human capital and benefit from their demographic dividend. Moreover, unlike developed countries they need to grow in an environmentally responsible and sustainable way. Developing countries have no choice but to adopt and generate new technologies and knowledge efficiently and effectively to deal with the many challenges of a rapidly changing global development context.

Numerous solutions exist to achieve these goals, but they are not always easy to find and put into action. Charting an innovation path requires thinking outside the box, and an ability to see change as an opportunity and not as a threat. To realize innovation opportunities, an organization must build its core values on the desire to create change that adds value. This is what drives the Asian Development Bank (ADB) to better serve its developing member countries (DMCs) in the 21st century.

The question is no longer if, but how ADB should advance the innovation agenda. This is clearly reflected in Strategy 2030, which articulates ADB's role in promoting, facilitating, and driving innovation.[2]

In December 2015, ADB approved $5 million for Knowledge and Support Technical Assistance 9017: Unlocking Innovation for Development. This technical assistance (TA) aims to strengthen the capacity of ADB's DMCs to solve development problems using innovative solutions. The TA project was divided into two parts: one to implement existing innovative solutions and the other to pilot new ideas crowdsourced from within the bank through an in-house innovation challenge.

Although the creation of the TA project preceded the launch of Strategy 2030, all of its activities and pilots reflect the operational priorities of the strategy and embody ADB's three guiding principles: a country-focused approach, promotion of innovative technology, and providing integrated solutions (Figure 1). As well as

---

[1] Vitasek K. Nobel Laureate Paul Romer: *The Path To Economic Growth And Innovation.* Forbes. Nov 19 2018. https://www.forbes.com/sites/katevitasek/2018/11/19/paul-romer-the-path-to-economic-growth-and-innovation/#22ab94c5139d Accessed February 14 2020.
E.D. Hess and R.K. Kazanjian, eds. 2006. *The Search for Organic Growth.* Cambridge: Cambridge University Press.
A. Saxenian. 1996. *Regional Advantage: Culture and Competition in Silicon Valley and Route 128.* Cambridge, MA: Harvard University Press.
R.R. Nelson, 1993. *National Innovation Systems: A Comparative Analysis.* New York: Oxford University Press.
[2] ADB. 2018. *Strategy 2030: Achieving a Prosperous, Inclusive, Resilient, and Sustainable Asia and the Pacific.* Manila.

being aligned with ADB's Strategy 2030 key operational priorities, in many cases they also supported countries as they strive to reach the 2030 Sustainable Development Goals (SDGs).

Why ADB Cares about Innovation

As a large operation, ADB needs to capture as many good ideas from within and also beyond the bank as possible. It is essential to understand what works, for whom, and in what circumstances. Armed with this information, ADB knows better what to take to scale, and how. It needs to be confident in its advocacy for innovative approaches in its DMCs so that it can support countries to try new things and break away from business as usual.

ADB is an organization with operations that straddle multiple major sectors and themes, from infrastructure to energy, from climate change to gender equity. There is power in being able to bring about cross-sector innovations. In addition, ADB can bring disparate parties together to work toward a common goal. To achieve this, it needs to foster innovative partnerships with the private sector. Sometimes the innovation is not the idea itself, but the introduction of an existing proven concept in a new environment where it has never been tested before.

The need for ADB to innovate and become stronger as a knowledge bank is woven into Strategy 2030. For example, the strategy commits ADB to proactively seek ways to promote the use of advanced technologies across its operations and provide capacity-building support to DMCs to do the same. Strategy 2030 also commits ADB to use its unique blend of private sector finance knowledge and deep sovereign relations to deliver innovative solutions for mobilizing finance from commercial sources. ADB can also use trust funds to promote innovation, enhance project quality, and provide critical support for innovative project implementation.

The Unlocking Innovation for Development TA project aimed to support all of these goals.

Unlocking Innovation for Development

At the five-year mark since the TA began, this report examines the evidence that has emerged so far to better understand in which ways the TA achieved its aims, and also what can be learned from the activities and pilots that did not go as planned. This introspection is well-timed, because it will inform how the innovation agenda of Strategy 2030 can be successfully implemented. This success will rely on systems thinking, a differentiated approach, and innovative partnerships, and this TA holds valuable lessons for all three.

When projects have been completed and positive results are visible, it is gratifying to look at what was successful. The temptation is always to downplay what did not work, and even sweep failure completely under the rug. But creating the conditions for successful innovation relies on a perhaps counterintuitive idea: there must be space for ideas to fail as well as succeed. While responsible stewardship of resources must always be maintained, no innovation can come from an environment where there is no tolerance for the risk that an idea might not work in practice. Innovation also means creating new ways within ADB for people to work together and collaborate, and this TA project supported that ideal.

The project was a mixed bag of disparate activities, some more successful than others. Through both the activities and the pilots, the project successfully financed a wide range of innovations, not just technological, but also in terms of governance, policy, and strategy to achieve development goals.

Sometimes the innovation is not the idea itself, but the introduction of an existing proven concept in a new environment where it has never been tested before.

Figure 1: ADB's Strategy 2030: Guiding Principles and Technical Assistance Outputs

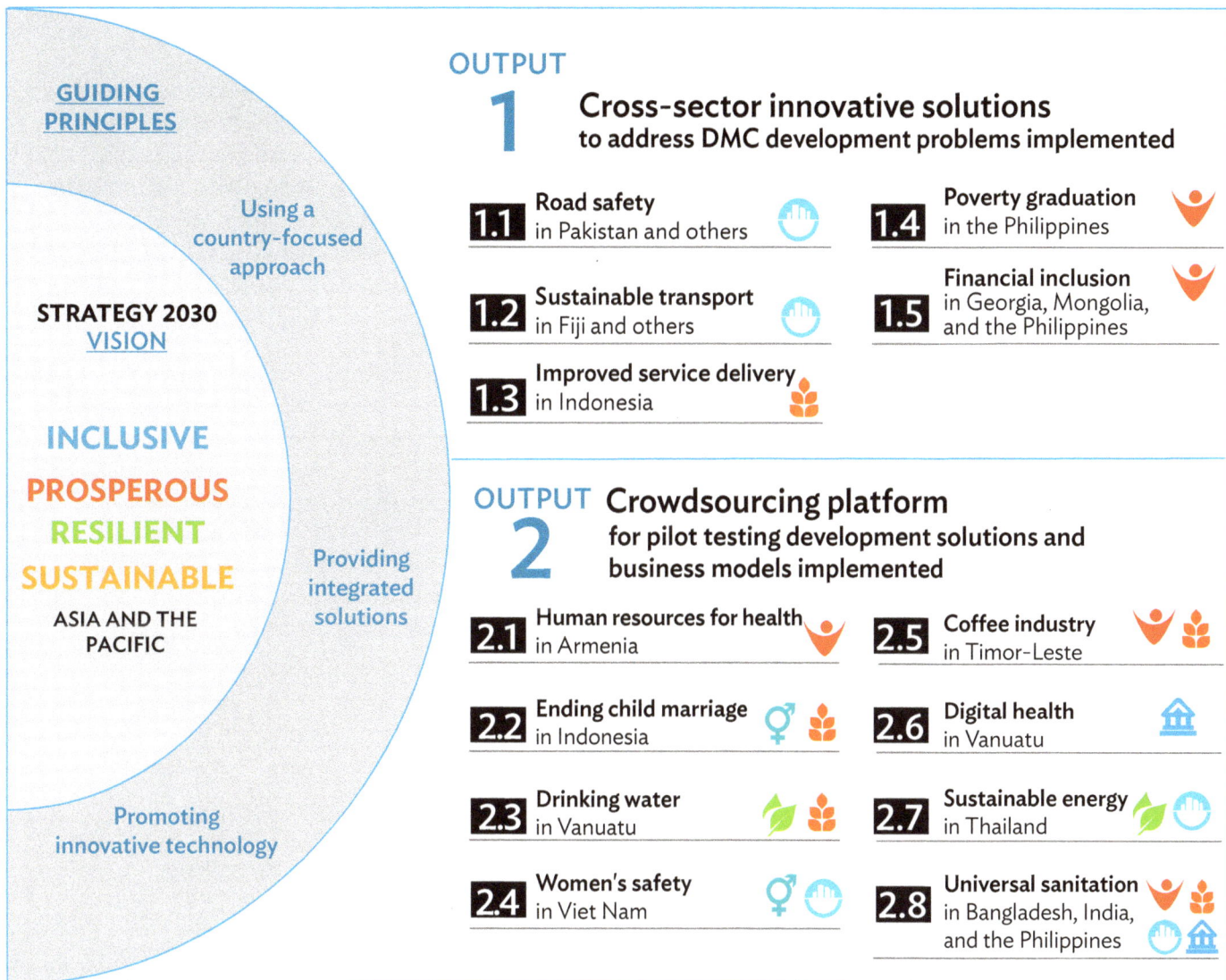

GUIDING PRINCIPLES

Using a country-focused approach

STRATEGY 2030 VISION

INCLUSIVE
PROSPEROUS
RESILIENT
SUSTAINABLE
ASIA AND THE PACIFIC

Providing integrated solutions

Promoting innovative technology

OUTPUT 1
Cross-sector innovative solutions
to address DMC development problems implemented

1.1 Road safety in Pakistan and others

1.2 Sustainable transport in Fiji and others

1.3 Improved service delivery in Indonesia

1.4 Poverty graduation in the Philippines

1.5 Financial inclusion in Georgia, Mongolia, and the Philippines

OUTPUT 2
Crowdsourcing platform
for pilot testing development solutions and business models implemented

2.1 Human resources for health in Armenia

2.2 Ending child marriage in Indonesia

2.3 Drinking water in Vanuatu

2.4 Women's safety in Viet Nam

2.5 Coffee industry in Timor-Leste

2.6 Digital health in Vanuatu

2.7 Sustainable energy in Thailand

2.8 Universal sanitation in Bangladesh, India, and the Philippines

ADB'S OPERATIONAL PRIORITIES

Addressing remaining poverty and reducing inequalities

Accelerating progress in gender equality

Tackling climate change, building climate and disaster resilience, and enhancing environmental sustainability

Making cities more livable

Promoting rural development and food security

Strengthening governance and institutional capacity

Fostering regional cooperation and integration

DMC = developing member country.
Source: Asian Development Bank.

IMPACT HIGHLIGHTS

How the Technical Assistance Project Was Structured

The project was divided into two parts: one comprised five activities that implemented innovations across sectors to address development challenges in DMCs. These activities supported the design and implementation of both ongoing and new loans. The second part comprised eight pilot projects that gave sector and thematic group project officers scope to try out new ideas nested within an existing project, extending the scope of what they could do within their existing resource envelopes.

The activities and pilots contributed to changes in policy and strategy, and also shifted the mindsets and behavior of stakeholders. Moreover, the TA project functioned as an advocacy tool, and acted as a catalyst for the mobilization of additional financial resources from within and beyond the bank. The implementers all reported that the activities and pilots had gained traction and produced results. While some did not reach their desired full potential, others did, and some exceeded expectations.

- In **Armenia**, the TA supported efforts to improve quality of care, and enabled ADB to establish a presence in the country as a partner in the health sector, which supported the subsequent development of a policy-based loan covering both education and health.
- In **Georgia**, a single, unified interface to a bank's applications improved its loan application system and made it more customer-centric.
- In **Indonesia**, a funded activity tested multistakeholder engagement mechanisms for complaint handling in the health and education sectors. Dashboards on child marriage were created to facilitate better understanding of its drivers, improve services to end it, monitor progress, and serve as an example of how achieving and monitoring the Sustainable Development Goals (SDGs) can be localized.
- In **Fiji**, **Malaysia**, and **Thailand**, action plans were developed for sustainable transport.
- In **Pakistan**, the fund was used to introduce engineers and consultants in road assessment and to develop a country-specific road assessment program.

- In the **Philippines**, an activity tried a new, more cost-effective way to deliver an already highly effective anti-poverty intervention, and another enabled a bank serving the poor to migrate to newer and more cost-efficient technology.
- A pilot in **Timor-Leste** created a reality TV program on best practices in coffee production, leading to entrepreneurial collaboration between coffee growers and baristas.
- Activities in **Vanuatu** piloted the use of solar panels to pull moisture from the air for clean water, and another devised a digital health strategy for the country.
- In **Viet Nam**, an ADB loan-funded transport infrastructure activity benefited from high-volume, reliable, crowdsourced, gender-sensitive urban audit data collected by young people to inform its support infrastructure planning process.

The activities and pilots contributed to changes in policy and strategy, and also shifted the mindsets and behavior of stakeholders.

Table 1: Contributions to Loans and Other Technical Assistance Projects

Subproject	Loan/Technical Assistance	Impact
Activity 1	**Loan 3574 (Pakistan):** Central Asia Regional Economic Cooperation Corridor Development Investment Program-Tranche 1 (approved Sep 2017)	Provided road safety input to the existing loan projects and establishing the Pakistan Road Assessment Program.
Activity 3	**TA 9288 (Regional):** Strengthening Government and Civil Society Cooperation and Civil Society Cooperation in Open Government Partnerships to Improve Public Services (approved Dec 2016)	Catalyzed TA funding of approximately $500,000 under TA 9288. Demonstrated how social accountability mechanisms can strengthen service delivery in health and education, informed dialogue for policy-based loans, and project replication supported by the Government of East Java.
Activity 4	**TA 9017 (Regional):** Unlocking Innovation for Development **TA 8332 (Regional):** Developing Impact Evaluation Methodologies, Approaches and Capacities **TA 9592 (Regional):** Deepening Civil Society Engagement for Development Effectiveness **TA 9534 (Regional):** Enhancing ADB Support for Social Protection to Achieve the SDGs	Catalyzed funding from three other sources within ADB (total $521,000) and then more than matched it with contributions worth $1.61 million from country counterparts to increase total funding from $720,000 to $2.85 million.
Activity 5	**TA 9170:** Promoting Smart Systems in ADB's Future Cities Program (approved Sep 2016) **Loan 46925-014 (Georgia):** TBC Bank Promoting Financial Sector Growth and Service Diversity (approved Jan 2013) **Loan 3072 (Mongolia):** Payment System Modernization Project (approved Nov 2013) **TA 9364:** Strengthening Financial Sector Operations in Asia and the Pacific **TA 9166 (Philippines):** Financial Inclusion Framework Strengthening (approved Aug 2016) Reducing Income Inequality through Financial Inclusion Program (pipeline)	Demonstrated how digital financial services can effectively serve the unbanked or underserved population by linking with ongoing projects from the ADB operations departments. Potential pilot projects have been identified based on the road map developed: i. Digitized field-based loan processing to increase access to finance rural small and medium-sized enterprises (SMEs) and smallholder farmers in Georgia; ii. Cloud-based shared platform to support nonbank financial institutions in Mongolia to digitize and automate customer onboarding and loan underwriting in a cost-efficient way while increasing their outreach; iii. Project performance of current local government; and iv. Sector project by applying digitized tax billing and payment system. In addition, the use of cloud-based core banking technology with a rural bank in the Philippines was piloted through the TA project. The shift is expected to bring a more flexible and accurate banking system given the reduced cost, leading to increased operational efficiency, increased convenience for customers, and ultimately boost financial inclusion.

Subproject	Loan/Technical Assistance	Impact
Pilot 1	**Proposed Loan 51129-002 (Armenia):** Social Sectors Reform Sovereign Project 1	Enabled ADB to establish a presence in Armenia as a partner in the health sector, which supported the subsequent development of a policy-based loan covering both education and health.
Pilot 2	**TA 9288 (Regional):** Strengthening Government and Civil Society Cooperation and Civil Society Cooperation in Open Government Partnerships to Improve Public Services (approved Dec 2016)	Developed a simple and practical manual on reproductive health and how to raise awareness and campaign to eliminate child marriage. Incorporated child marriage research questions and progress indicators in the replication of community complaint handling mechanisms. Led to local governments' budgeting for dashboard software in next year's budget and discussion in the use of data dashboards for other sectors.
Pilot 4	**TA 9561 (India):** Strengthening the Capacity of Kolkata Municipal Corporation for Resilient Urban Services	Safetipin, a personal safety app, hired as social vulnerability audit expert to collect and code vulnerability-related geotagged information.
Pilot 5	**TA 50334-001 (Timor-Leste):** Support for Preparation of a National Coffee Sector Development Plan	Contributed to the visibility of the Timor-Leste Coffee Association as a key stakeholder in the development and implementation of the sector development plan.
Pilot 6	**Proposed Loan/Grant 50282-001:** Regional Health Systems Strengthening for Effective Coverage of New Vaccines in the Pacific Project	Improved the digital health system in Vanuatu, which will also improve the vaccination information system.

ADB = Asian Development Bank, TA = technical assistance.
Source: Asian Development Bank.

Figure 2: Technical Assistance Projects and Thematic Areas

Sustainable transport

1.1 Scaling Up Innovative Road Safety Operations in Pakistan and Other Countries
Trained Pakistan engineers and consultants in road assessment, using the International Road Assessment Programme model and its expertise.

1.2 Scaling Up Innovative Urban Transport Operations in Fiji and Other Countries
Developed action plans for sustainable transport (involving traffic planning, pedestrians, and public transport) in Fiji, as well as five Southeast Asian cities.

2.4 "Safetipin" for Women's Safety in Viet Nam
Used a personal safety app where high-volume, reliable, crowdsourced, gender-sensitive urban audit data supported the infrastructure planning process. It also increased social accountability, and demonstrated the unique role that youth-led projects can play in this.

Health

1.3 Consolidating and Replicating Innovative Service Delivery Practices in Districts in Indonesia
Made measurable improvements to the education and health-care-related public service complaints mechanism and made a strong case for scale-up and replication. It was replicated in two districts.

2.1 Human Resources for Integrated Health-Care Delivery in Armenia
Mapped out future trends in human resources for health, together with Armenia's Ministry of Health.

2.3 Pulling Moisture from the Atmosphere for Clean Drinking Water in Vanuatu
Piloted the use of moisture from the atmosphere that allowed a community to have clean drinking water. The equipment supplier has used the pilot as a test case for expansion into remote areas.

2.6 Developing a Digital Health Strategy in Vanuatu
Avoided fragmentation of the health information systems and promoted implementation of single-entry, multiple use data collection.

2.8 Toilet Board Coalition's Toilet Accelerator Program in Bangladesh, India, and the Philippines
Tested the mechanism for engaging an external partner to pilot a toilet accelerator program innovation on a small-scale basis in Bangladesh, India, and the Philippines.

Social development

1.4 Applying Graduation Programs to End Extreme Poverty in the Philippines
Provided data for cost-effective decision-making for an intervention that is proven to be highly effective, but which has high start-up costs.

Economic empowerment

1.5 **Scaling Up Financial Inclusion through Digital Financial Services Systems in Georgia, Mongolia, and the Philippines**

Enabled a bank operating in low-access provinces to extend operations beyond bricks-and-mortar branches and increase financial inclusion, especially of the unbanked.

2.5 **Reality TV Program on Best Practices in Coffee Production in Timor-Leste**

Produced a reality TV program that helped improve coffee production quality. The pilot accelerated the emergence of a group of young Timorese coffee entrepreneurs.

Women empowerment

2.2 **Dashboard on Child Marriage in Indonesia**

Created dashboards that allowed government, religious leaders, and civil society access to data that had never been compiled to look at the issue of child marriage in an accessible, highly visual form that can be easily updated to show progress toward ending child marriage.

Sustainable energy

2.7 **Creating an Innovative Utility Energy Services Model in Thailand**

Due to begin in early 2020.

Source: Asian Development Bank.

Table 2: Regional and Country-Level Impact

Primary

- Armenia
- Bangladesh
- Fiji
- Georgia
- India
- Indonesia
- Pakistan
- Philippines
- Thailand
- Timor-Leste
- Vanuatu
- Viet Nam

Secondary

- Lao People's Democratic Republic
- Malaysia
- Maldives
- Mongolia
- Myanmar
- People's Republic of China

Source: Asian Development Bank.

KEY LESSONS LEARNED

1 | **Innovation has to be intentional, not for its own sake**

Innovation should be anchored to a specific need in the country concerned. It is crucial to clearly identify the problem to be solved or what can be done better. Successful innovations, although novel, are not without scientific basis. In the development context, they must have a practical intention.

For example, in the Philippines, when Cantilan Bank introduced cloud-based core banking, it significantly reduced operational costs, which in turn enabled the bank to better serve rural customers. Similarly, when FINCA Bank Georgia introduced a united front-end solution—a single, unified interface to all banking applications—to improve its loan application system and make it more customer-centric, three key performance indicators had to be met for the project to go ahead: reduced transaction costs, reduced staff time required, and shorter transaction times.

2 | **Buy-in can make or break an innovation**

Buy-in from counterparts, especially government agencies, makes or breaks a project. In Indonesia, the Child Marriage Dashboard pilot enjoyed significant local government buy-in. This sense of ownership had been carefully cultivated over many years. Moreover, alignment with existing policy objectives was crucial. The multistakeholder approach that was adopted went far beyond the usual "counterpart" concept and even involved religious courts. Government officials at multiple levels (provincial and local), including judiciary partners (religious courts) and civil society, were keen to improve development indicators and tackle child marriage for an array of reasons, including child protection, girls' rights, and for educational and economic reasons, so they were enthusiastic about the project.

If buy-in is in name only, or absent, or withdrawn due to a change in political leadership, it can severely undermine or even end a project. In the Philippines poverty graduation activity, for example, while implementation was in progress, the counterpart agency (the Department of Social Welfare and Development) backed out due to a change in administration and in priorities. This resulted

in delays to implementation. Similarly, in Pakistan, where a comparable activity was due to begin, the activity has struggled to get support from the counterpart agency (Benazir Income Support Programme). Even with the counterpart agency's commitment, the activity had to be cancelled.

3 | **ADB's internal process can be the dead hand of bureaucracy to a small, innovative project**

ADB's standard processes, which have been developed over time and refined to fit the needs of large projects such as infrastructure development, are sometimes too cumbersome for small innovation projects, leading to implementation delays that compromise their efficiency. Several activities under the Unlocking Innovation for Development TA projects reported delays in, for example, hiring consultants, funding workshops run by national consultants, contracting civil society organizations, or releasing funds, and at times experienced almost fatal complications when trying to run innovative activities within existing ADB systems.

Real innovation funding needs more flexible procurement rules and incentives for private sector and civil society partners to collaborate. It is also necessary to put in place contingencies to ensure continuity of implementation even if the project leads change. All these factors support the need for a dedicated innovation team in the bank to support staff to innovate.

4 | **Pilots need to be given both time and money to flourish, and then scaled**

Piloting is necessary to see interventions firsthand and learn about their benefits and shortcomings. Initial scoping does not always lead in the right direction, and new ideas need flexibility for a more iterative experimentation process to unfold. This takes time, and meaningful results, even for a small-scale project, cannot always be achieved in a span of 1 year.

For example, the TV show in Timor-Leste had high production values relative to its shoestring budget but would have had more impact if coupled with an extensive social media campaign, which was beyond the scope of the pilot budget. Similarly, the crowdsourced data collection pilot in Viet Nam would have been faster and more impactful if data has been collected by paid participants rather than volunteers. To really benefit from an innovative pilot, there should be time and scope for successful ones to be taken to scale. In the case of the cloud-based core banking pilot in the Philippines, working with a cloud-based Software as a Service (SaaS) and a service provider in a different time zone can be challenging, especially during technically intense periods. While the service provider factored in ample support during implementation, the extent of required support was underestimated. Also, the longer-than-expected transition process—operating old and new systems in parallel for more than a year—resulted in considerably higher workloads than foreseen. The Cantilan pilot team would have benefited from creating a slightly larger team as well as appointing champions at selected branches or cluster of branches at an earlier stage.

Successful innovations, although novel, are not without scientific basis. In the development context, they must have a practical intention.

SUSTAINABLE TRANSPORT

1.1

Scaling Up Innovative Road Safety Operations

Innovative ways to make roads safer

By the time the TA project was set up, it was becoming apparent that demand for traditional transport projects was likely to decrease, and at the same time demand for new ways of working to improve transport would increase. Globally, the trend is toward transport management, better planning, and maintenance rather than simply increasing the quantity of roads.

The challenge

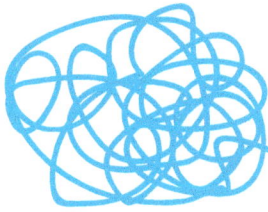

The innovation

Making safety a priority in Pakistan transport projects

For the past decade, ADB's work in the transport sector has focused on creating systems that are accessible, affordable, environment-friendly, and safe. It can be challenging to ensure that safety is more than a buzzword in project planning and given the attention it deserves. With this in mind, $750,000 of the bank's innovation funding was deployed to scale up innovative road safety operations, notably in Pakistan.

Using a geographic information system platform to assess road safety

ADB engaged the nongovernmental organization International Road Assessment Programme (iRAP) to conduct safety assessments for projects under five ADB loans worth over $60 million in Georgia, the Lao People's Democratic Republic, Mongolia, Pakistan, and Viet Nam.

The team has directly supported regional operations in the transport sector through road safety assessment activities that influenced the design and implementation of ADB-financed transport projects. In Pakistan, the TA was used to train engineers and consultants in road assessment, using the iRAP model to develop the Pakistan Road Assessment Program (PAKRAP 2017–2019). This will support road safety activities by Pakistan's National Highway Authority and enable large-scale road assessments and promote the cause of road safety.

Learning point

What went well

The innovation team worked opportunistically with project officers to add a road safety dimension to road projects that otherwise would be absent from project design and implementation.

What could have been better

The scoping and selection of projects for activity assistance can be a hit-or-miss situation, and in this project, it contributed to the delay in hiring consultants. There was initial uncertainty on whether to adopt knowledge partnership or consulting services as the modality of engagement.

To take the innovation further, a geographic information system platform such as the one used in this activity can include a layer to assess the health effects associated with the severity of transport injuries and existing access to urgent surgical care, which can then feed into projects under the health sector, a prime example of how the innovation fund can promote cross-sector initiatives.

Scaling Up Innovative Urban Transport Operations

Short-term goals with real results

The challenge

The innovation

Scaling up innovative urban transport operations in Fiji, Malaysia, and Thailand

In sustainable transport, the policy innovation is making transport systems more people-oriented and less focused on the vehicle. This $750,000 activity set out to scale up what works in Fiji and also in five Asian cities, all of which are major tourist destinations: Krabi, Langkawi, Melaka, Penang, and Phuket. In Malaysia and Thailand, it piggybacked existing TA projects associated with the Indonesia–Malaysia–Thailand Growth Triangle, a subregional cooperation initiative formed in 1993 by the governments of Indonesia, Malaysia, and Thailand to accelerate economic and social transformation in less developed provinces.

IT-enabled sustainable development plans

Using innovation funding, ADB developed action plans for sustainable transport, involving traffic planning, pedestrians, and public transport. The activity also worked in Suva, Fiji to develop an action plan for urban transport and renewal of outdated buses. The plan equipped the Government of Fiji with a blueprint to implement improvements to public transport, traffic management to optimize the use of existing transport infrastructure, parking management, and promotion of walking and cycling. Assessment of the existing bus fleet found that 700 of the more than 1,600 buses in use in Fiji do not have any emissions standards, and 400 buses are at least 30 years old. Accessibility is also an issue with older buses, and with the main bus terminals.

Unlocking Innovation for Development supported ADB road projects to ensure they have a traffic safety component integrated in a systematic manner. The TA project enabled the project officers to engage the city governments in dialogue and within a tight time frame, produce action plans for sustainable transport that looked at public transport, pedestrianization, and traffic management, and brought in international external experts to work alongside ADB staff and country counterparts. The innovation was an effective policy dialogue, which leads to inclusion of road safety measures in national transport planning.

By combining an innovative approach and technology, the activity influenced the design and implementation of ADB-financed transport projects. It ensured that ADB developed a holistic urban transport system assessment for its existing projects and directly supported regional operations on the transport sector.

Learning point

What went well

By contributing to better transport planning in key tourist cities, providing vital inputs to support project preparation and implementation in areas with newly introduced urban transport, the project gave initial quality assurance for urban transport projects. It also enabled ADB to explore new business opportunities for expanding urban transport lending.

Safetipin App in Viet Nam

Where there is youth, there is data

The challenge

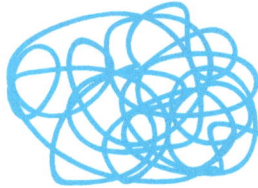

The innovation

Gender-sensitive infrastructure planning in Viet Nam

Through a $58.95 million loan, ADB is helping Viet Nam upgrade facilities for users of stations along Ha Noi's metro line 3 railway.[3] The project comprises construction of pedestrian subways, bus stops, and other physical assets to help metro users get in and out of stations quickly and safely. This complements ADB support for construction of the metro line itself. However, detailed, gender-sensitive audit data were missing. These were needed to inform its support infrastructure planning process and to ensure that construction of these assets took safety for women fully into account.

Crowdsourcing audit data

The pilot conducted gender-sensitive safety audits by young people using the smartphone app, Safetipin, to crowdsource data on urban safety. The pilot was designed and managed by ADB's Youth for Asia program, which supports young people in contributing effectively to development by mainstreaming youth participation in ADB operations, partnering on the ground with the Viet Nam branch of AIESEC, the world's largest youth-run international nongovernment organization.

ADB conducted awareness-raising and capacity-building activities using both online and offline platforms, and over a 6-week period in 2018 collected data. For example, when a participant saw an area that was poorly lit, he or she could report that through the Safetipin Nite application safety audit, which consists of a set of nine parameters that together contribute to the perception of safety, with data geo-located and compiled to generate a safety score. This generated high-volume, reliable, crowdsourced, gender-sensitive urban audit data, which were also publicly available.

The pilot demonstrated how crowdsourced data can help guide public projects, and can be generated quickly. It also piloted an app that has wide applicability across other sectors and shed light on the potential for a public–private partnership with the app developer. This pilot also showed the young people's flexibility in dealing with diverse partners, as they reached out to the elderly, people with disabilities, and women's groups.

Learning point

What went well

This was a model of inclusion—with the involvement of young people contributing to social accountability through technology, which can be replicated in other contexts and sectors wherever good data are needed, or to hold the relevant government agencies to account.

What could have been better

The pilot was added to the infrastructure project either too soon or too late: it could have been more effective if it had been introduced either at the metro design stage, or once the metro system was already in use. There were also language barriers, and the pilot would have benefited from a local lead who could communicate more easily with government counterparts. Relying on volunteers also diluted the impact and created a lack of momentum, so a pilot which should have been completed in 3 months ended up being spread out over a year.

---

[3] ADB. 2014. *Report and Recommendation of the President to the Board of Directors: Proposed Loans to Viet Nam for Strengthening Sustainable Urban Transport for Ha Noi Metro Line 3.* Manila. https://www.adb.org/projects/40080-024/main

"

The initiative has raised the awareness of gender and safety for young people and the Government of Viet Nam in a more comprehensive way. In particular, the Safetipin application allows everyone to take part in developing a safer environment for themselves and their family. Besides, the government could use the data generated by Safetipin as a reference source to improve traffic organization and enhance people's safety.

"

Pham Thi Ngoc Linh
Official, Ha Noi Transport and Investment Management Unit

HEALTH

1.3

Consolidating and Replicating Innovative Service Delivery Practices in Districts in Indonesia

Service excellence in the public sector

The challenge

The innovation

Accountable public service delivery in Indonesia

Between 2010 and 2015, with funding from the United States Agency for International Development, RTI International implemented its Local Governance Service Improvement program (Kinerja) in 79 districts across five provinces in Indonesia. When the project came to an end, it was clear that most actively involved districts could benefit from ongoing support to address supply and demand side constraints in improving basic public service delivery, and strengthened accountability mechanisms.

Empowering staff to be more responsive and improve quality of care

This activity worked with public service staff and citizens in the health and education sectors. In health, one of the activity's most popular trainings was on improving frontline services through redefining self-image, which was credited with changing mindsets and improving attitudes and teamwork. There were workshops for community health center staff on implementation of standard operating procedures and better use of the client complaints process to improve services. Multistakeholder forums helped community health centers to develop service charters to respond to problems identified in complaint surveys. The centers had never run anything like this before and were in fact apprehensive about the idea at first, but have since embraced the value of an effective complaint mechanism. Training on maternal mortality social autopsy helped community health centers improve their ability to discover the root social, cultural, religious, and economic problems behind maternal deaths.

In education, the activity supported implementation of public service-oriented school-based management in 30 schools. Having already begun the process of conducting a complaint survey under the United States Agency for International Development project, this activity continued to support the schools as they developed their service charters and technical recommendations.

Because it built on a previous project, this initiative capitalized on existing relationships, and had very strong buy-in from provincial and district governments. With a budget of $1 million, and focused on four districts in East Java, the pilot project was intended to feed into the preparation of a policy-based loan for local government service delivery and to inform knowledge management functions by ADB's Governance Thematic Group.

Learning point

What went well

The activity made measurable improvements to education and health-care-related public services through developing a complaints mechanism, and led to significant local scale-up and replication. It successfully created a complaint handling system that aligns with the country's law on public services and reforms. The activity also mobilized additional resources, with local governments committing just over $129,000 in counterpart funding to replicate the innovation at selected districts and provinces.

Because the team members were working with previously-trained local government staff and community members, the project's speed and success was enhanced. The project self-replicated in 14 other community health centers with their own local budget and internal facilitator team.

What could have been better

The demand for replication of the project activities far outstripped available funding. Time constraints on team members meant that there was insufficient documentation of the innovations and their impact. If the activities had been implemented across more sites simultaneously it would have helped make an even stronger case for wider scale-up. It would have been better to expand government involvement from the District Health Office and BAPPEDA (District Planning and Development Office) to more institutions such as the District Tourism Office.

"

The community complaint concept from the program is extraordinary. Our community health center is currently undergoing the accreditation process, and as the head, I need this sort of feedback so we can improve services. If we link the community complaint survey to the accreditation process, they match well, because for the accreditation requirements, the planning aspect should also explore the community's inputs. Previously, we used to get community feedback through SMS, complaint boxes, or WhatsApp, but now with the multistakeholder forum involving the community in complaint surveys, there is additional valuable input that helps us progress towards accreditation.

"

Rini Endrawati
Doctor and Head of Bubakan Community Health Center, Pacitan

2.1
Human Resources Work Under an Integrated Health-Care Delivery in Armenia

Building better health-care from the bottom up

The challenge

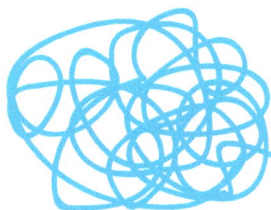

The innovation

Reforming health services and increasing coverage in Armenia

Armenia's health service is plagued by low-quality service delivery, poor responsiveness to patient needs, and inadequate systems for facilities licensing and continuing education of health-care workers. Health-care is publicly funded, but curative care is only provided free of charge to the poor, vulnerable, and special categories, including children below the age of 7 years. Co-payments are typically 50% of the cost, far above the maximum 30% threshold that is considered essential to ensure universal health coverage. Although there is a nationwide electronic medical records system in place, patient data collection mechanisms are weak and not integrated.

Evidence-informed decisions to get social health insurance right

Through an innovation pilot, ADB worked with Armenia's Ministry of Health to map future trends in human resources for health: although there is currently a surplus of doctors, for example, the aging population will mean that many doctors will reach retirement just as the population's health-care needs increase. Armenia will face a shortage, not a surplus, unless it plans for its future human resources for health needs in advance.

ADB developed two dynamic tools to help ensure the ministry is making evidence-informed planning decisions, one for human resources for health and the other an actuarial tool for overall health-care financing. The tools are both Excel-based, meaning every calculation is visible, and there are no "black box" features. Ministry staff were also trained to use such decision tools.

ADB provided international and national expert technical assistance to analyze the rationalization efforts in Armenia in the past 7 years, as well as analyze the primary health-care, hospital services, and the health workforce demands. Norms from Baltic states and other countries in the region, such as on the optimal number of doctors per 1,000 population, gave the government helpful points of comparison, and a study tour to Estonia helped them determine priorities for Armenia's health system.

Learning point

What went well

Having access to relatively small amounts of funding such as this pilot TA project enabled ADB to demonstrate to the Government of Armenia that it was a valuable partner in the health sector, which had never been on the country's agenda before with regard to accessing ADB financing. As a result of the pilot, ADB has become well-positioned to be a trusted partner of the government to address its double burden of noncommunicable diseases and population aging. The goodwill and relationships established over 2 years supported the subsequent inclusion of health in a $10 million policy-based loan for the Human Development Enhancement Program. That program supports the necessary reforms to improve the education and health services, providing the foundation for the government's planned increased investment in human development.

What could have been better

A revolution in Armenia resulted in a complete change of direction for the Ministry of Health, and the project had to adapt accordingly. Although the grant funding was relatively easy to secure, the micromanagement of how it was disbursed when the scope of work had to change created an administrative burden for the team that far outweighed the level of funding. Having a defined output, and giving autonomy to the TA project recipients as to how that output was achieved, would have been a better approach.

2.3
Pulling Moisture from the Atmosphere for Clean Drinking Water in Vanuatu

Water out of thin air

The challenge

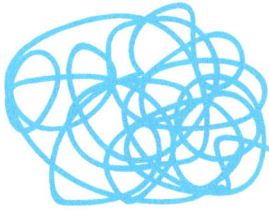

The innovation

Improving water quality in a remote area of Vanuatu

After Cyclone Pam devastated Vanuatu in 2015, ADB engaged on a cyclone recovery project. One of the project sites, Tanna, sits in the shadow of an active volcano. Its continuous eruptions send sulfur-laden dust into the air, which impacts the surface water, causing acid rain. This is a real constraint to drinking water in communities close to the volcano, and ADB was interested in a new technology that uses solar panels, which can pull moisture from the atmosphere and convert this to clean drinking water.

Solar-powered atmospheric water generators

ADB piloted solar-powered atmospheric water generators at a small school close to a location where the bank was already working. If the project works, it not only provides a community with clean drinking water, but also gives the equipment supplier a test case for expansion into remote areas.

ADB funding paid for the installation of 20 solar-powered atmospheric water generator units to augment drinking water over a period spanning the system's estimated economic life of 15 years.

Though at slightly less capacity than expected, the panels are working and the water meets and exceeds the World Health Organization (WHO) water quality guidelines to a greater extent than existing water sources from rainwater and a nearby spring. The water produced is fully utilized, both by the school where the facility has been installed and the nearby medical center staff. There has been strong buy-in from the local community, which used its own resources to build a fence around the facility when there was no money left in the pilot budget.

Learning point

What went well

For both the government and community, the pilot demonstrates a new form of water collection technology that addresses a pressing development issue in Vanuatu. For the equipment supplier, it created an opportunity to install the technology in a location they otherwise would not have accessed. It is a test case for them as to how to make a business case for expanding their market to remote locations, especially in terms of ongoing maintenance. The generators produced water that was of a higher standard than existing sources.

The as-yet unanswered question is: what would be the cost recovery model for a scaled-up version of the pilot? Structural concrete works, transport, and installation are expensive in remote Tanna, and therefore cost was significantly more than originally anticipated: $28,000 vs. the $10,000 originally budgeted. This is especially pertinent when the average production over the 120-day evaluation period was 2.1 liters per day vs. the potential to produce 3–5 liters per day claimed by the manufacturer.

Digital Health Strategy in Vanuatu

A sustainable, integrated digital health system

The challenge

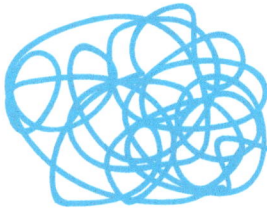

The innovation

Avoiding fragmentation in e-Health solutions in Vanuatu

Like many countries in Asia and the Pacific, Vanuatu recognizes the transformative role that digital health, also called e-Health, solutions can have in a health system. Digital health is defined by WHO as "the combined use of electronic communication and information technology in the health sector."[4] Practically speaking, this entails ensuring that the right person gets the right health information at the right time in a secure electronic form to support the delivery of quality and efficient health-care. The risk when countries begin to introduce digital health solutions is that a patchwork of applications creates a fragmented system, which does not deliver improved health outcomes.

A digital health strategy

With innovation funding, ADB worked with Vanuatu to develop its digital health strategy to ensure that there was strong governance in place at the outset so that information systems are integrated and do not overlap, and that data is not siloed where it is collected. Integration of data reporting through information and communication technology (ICT) enabled reporting at the service provision level, and resulted in improved financial management, use of digital payments, and improved accountability for quality service delivery.

Working together with WHO, which had earlier supported Vanuatu's Hospital Information Management System, ADB's project consultant used a participatory approach to create a strategy for a digital health information system that is integrated, streamlined, and sustainable. This will ensure that health information is not split between primary care and hospital settings, and that ICT projects are focused on country needs rather than driven by external priorities. The pilot delivered a draft digital health strategy with a 3-year implementation road map, with data entered through a tablet-based system that collects data from a single source and makes them available to multiple users within the health system.

Working on the draft strategy entailed in-depth assessment of required data management and service delivery processes for immunization and basic health-care delivery programs, including all information management and data entry levels, from the health worker to the health-care center, district hospital, and Ministry of Health. The pilot was linked to a $25 million ADB loan and grant, Regional Health Systems Strengthening for Effective Coverage of New Vaccines in the Pacific Project. This project formed part of the regional response to reduce the number of cervical cancer cases and infectious diseases in children and women through the introduction of new vaccines and early detection.

Improving the digital health system in Vanuatu will also improve the vaccination information system. Thus, rather than working on only one function of the health information system, the vaccine information system, the project helps address the root causes of weak information system management through the digital health strategy.

---

[4] WHO. *eHealth at WHO*. https://www.who.int/ehealth/about/en/

Learning point

What went well

Real innovation happens not in one sector or under one theme, but when it connects multiple sectors and stakeholders. The pilot played to ADB's strengths as a convener of multiple partners who otherwise would not necessarily connect and collaborate with each other, including development agencies, the government, the private sector, civil society, and nongovernment organizations.

What could have been better

It would have been better to link the digital health strategy with an investment case for digital health. The project could have capitalized more on the momentum of the participatory approach in developing the strategy and linking this project to larger capacity development efforts for health information system management together with WHO.

2.8
Toilet Board Coalition Toilet Accelerator Program

Bringing development partners and sanitation entrepreneurs together

The challenge

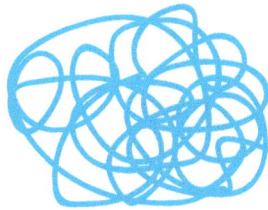

The innovation

Partnering with the private sector to accelerate access to sanitation

Although in the development sector, sanitation is typically categorized as a public service, sanitation is also a multibillion-dollar business. As a development partner, ADB has access to governments and implementation agencies and the capacity to scale good ideas with potential to achieve development goals. For its part, the private sector has invaluable expertise, both in cost-efficient product design, and in how to reach the poorest households. The challenge is finding a mechanism through which both parties together can achieve a common goal: Sustainable Development Goal 6 (SDG 6), universal access to sanitation.

Supporting the Toilet Board Coalition's work in Asia

The Toilet Board Coalition (TBC) is a business-led partnership and platform enabling private sector engagement and close collaboration between private, public, and nonprofit sectors. The TBC's Toilet Accelerator Program supports sanitation economy entrepreneurs to bring to fruition commercially viable innovations.

ADB signed a letter of agreement with the TBC to work together. The innovation pilot included pilot projects in Bangladesh, India, and the Philippines, where the TBC has supported businesses through its Toilet Accelerator program.

Learning point

What went well

By staying engaged despite internal process obstacles that made it difficult to do so, ADB has gained a valuable partner in the sanitation sector. The pilot created a mechanism through which ADB could build a partnership that otherwise would not have come about.

What could have been better

By being too wary of engaging with the private sector in what was traditionally for the bank a public sector enterprise, ADB missed out on the opportunity to shape the TBC agenda at the outset in accordance with ADB's poverty eradication mission. Now that the TBC has already matured, the window of opportunity for that influence has closed. The time lag from application to signing the letter of agreement with the TBC—16 months—was also unreasonably long.

SOCIAL DEVELOPMENT

Applying Graduation Programs to End Extreme Poverty in Philippines

Modest technical assistance with big impact

The challenge

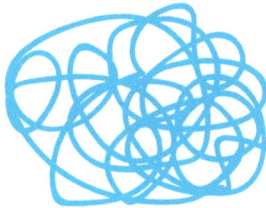

The innovation

A cost-effective intervention to tackle extreme poverty in the Philippines

The BRAC Ultra-Poor Graduation initiative is well-established as an innovative and effective way to help the extremely poor on the road to a sustained upward trajectory. However, the approach is expensive, not least because it comprises regular individual coaching to provide tailored solutions to business and personal issues (Figure 3). It is a resource-intensive approach, both in terms of human resources as well as cash and assets.

The challenge was how to introduce this program to recipients of the Philippines conditional cash transfer program Pantawid Pamilyang Pilipino Program (4Ps) in a way that was cost-effective and sustainable.

Piloting group coaching interventions

The activity recruited 2,400 4Ps recipients in Negros Oriental and divided them into four equal groups, one acting as a control group and the other three receiving different interventions: One group receives individual assets worth $300 per person (e.g., a pig and feed, a freezer and start-up stock, a massage kit) and group coaching from a trained graduation community facilitator; a second group receives group assets worth $6,000 per group of approximately 20 individuals plus group coaching; and a third group receives individual assets and personal coaching. All coaching occurs every 2 weeks, and all intervention groups receive skills training, savings facilitation, and community mobilization interventions.

Implemented by the Department of Labor and Employment with technical support from BRAC, and impact evaluation from Innovations for Poverty Action, the project runs from July 2018 to June 2020. It benefits from the region's uniquely rich pool of community-based social workers who serve as program

Figure 3: The BRAC Graduation Approach

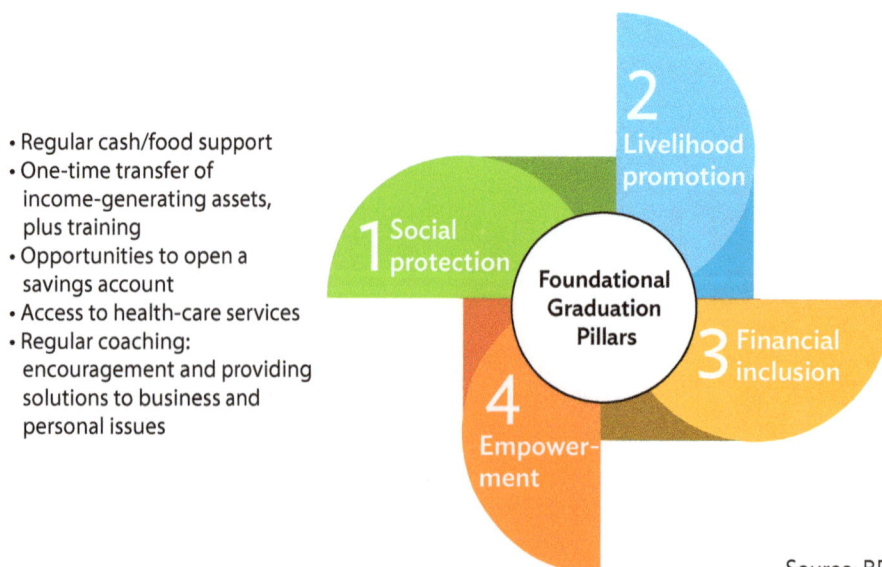

- Regular cash/food support
- One-time transfer of income-generating assets, plus training
- Opportunities to open a savings account
- Access to health-care services
- Regular coaching: encouragement and providing solutions to business and personal issues

1 Social protection

2 Livelihood promotion

Foundational Graduation Pillars

3 Financial inclusion

4 Empower-ment

Source: BRAC.

facilitators, and who can call on their strong grassroots knowledge and reputation.

The activity introduced the Graduation Approach to the Department of Labor and Employment, and the Department of Social Work and Development, which administers 4Ps project, and provided evidence for cost-effective decision-making. The activity is also testing a cheaper modality through group-based intervention, which is of significant interest to the global graduation community of practice. In addition, it combined funding from three other ADB TA funds and significant cofinancing from the government. The program brings together the Department of Labor and Employment's Integrated Livelihood Program, and the department committed $360,000 in counterpart funding for the asset transfer component for 1,200 households, as well as the conditional cash transfer component.

Knowledge from this activity can be transferred to other contexts: the approach has been taken up in other areas of ADB—the Philippines country office is seeking funding to implement the graduation approach in the context of urban involuntary resettlement in both the Philippines and India. Resettlement is an area where this approach has a lot of promise in ADB because a significant proportion of its investments entail resettlement. The coaching element in this activity is particularly helpful in the context of resettlement because it is so impactful through confidence it builds and the community cohesion it fosters.

Learning point

What went well

The initial $520,000 that was allocated to this activity catalyzed further funding from three other TA projects that doubled the resources available for this activity. It was more than doubled again by over $1.6 million in counterpart assets and cash contributions. With an additional $200,000 allocated from the Unlocking Innovation for Development TA in late August 2019, the activity was extended to June 2020; it has a total budget of nearly $2.85 million. Although delays in the distribution of assets to beneficiaries using government procurement processes have inevitably led to some attrition, taking the pace that the government counterparts could manage and patiently building trust with them has secured strong buy-in, which augurs well for getting beyond a successful pilot to scale-up.

What could have been better

The 2016 change of government resulted in new priorities in the original partner agency. It took time to redesign and start the activity with the new partner. The lesson for future projects of this kind was that some flexibility has to be built in at the start to allow for unforeseen changes, either to the project itself or to the partners ADB works with.

ECONOMIC EMPOWERMENT

Scaling Up Financial Inclusion through Digital Financial Services Systems

Going beyond bricks and mortar to reach the unbanked

The challenge

The innovation

Increasing financial inclusion in the Philippines

The vast majority of banking in the Philippines—over 90% of domestic deposits and 97% of loans—occurs in the 27 provinces with high access to bricks-and-mortar banks. However, a considerable number of locations lack access to banking services, and these areas have not attracted investments from the country's major banks. Cantilan Bank, Inc. on the other hand, had opened 24 branches and 19 extension offices covering 12 provinces in eastern Mindanao and Visayas by the end of 2017.

In the Caraga region, where much of Cantilan's presence is centered, the average family poverty incidence is over 30%, compared with 16.5 % nationwide, and approximately one in four families are unbanked. With 7 out of 10 adults keeping their savings at home, and informal borrowing the norm, areas such as this are ripe for innovative banking solutions that making banking services more efficient and cost-effective.

Cloud-banking technology

ADB worked with Cantilan to switch to full reliance on a cloud-based SaaS system in January 2019. With full migration to cloud-based banking, the expected outcomes were cost savings due to operational efficacy, creating greater impetus for inclusion of currently unbanked households in the banking system.

Despite delays and hiccups along the way, the promised benefits in terms of operational efficiency have been realized. On the banking side, the activity achieved its aim, although it is still too soon to assess the downstream impact on clients.

The activity's influence has also extended beyond the Philippines, with similar projects nested within loans to modernize the banking system in Georgia and Mongolia. The activity supported FINCA Bank Georgia to introduce a united front-end solution—a single, unified interface to all banking applications—to improve its loan application system and make it more customer-centric. In Mongolia, the activity included a pilot of a shared digital platform for nonbank financial institutions, to reduce operational costs and improve transaction speed and efficiency. Similarly, activities on the integration of noncash payment solutions have been included in the regional ADB-financed project, Promoting Smart Systems in ADB's Future Cities Program.

Learning point

What went well

Time and resources invested in building the business case, together with buy-in from senior management and formation of a dedicated team of Instafin Champions at an early stage, contributed to the team's ability to drive implementation forward, notably when facing unexpected challenges. Without these, it would likely have taken even longer to implement, or failed. The coalition of partners with aligned strategic visions contributed to overcoming key challenges that caused the longer phase of running the old and new systems in parallel.

The activity was also useful for banking regulator Bangko Sentral ng Pilipinas, which had put it in a regulatory sandbox while related regulations and processes were updated.

What could have been better

Had ADB processes and guidelines been clearer and not as stringent, it would have made the activity run more smoothly. It was difficult to fit it into existing and rigid project definitions.

Building-in time allowance for the unknown into the implementation schedule may have led to a more realistic timeline. Working with a cloud-based SaaS system and a service provider in a different time zone can be challenging, especially during technically intense periods. The service provider factored in ample support during implementation, but the extent of required support was underestimated.

Working with a service provider as a committed and responsive partner rather than seeing the system change as mere procurement was essential to overcome this issue. Continuous training to ensure effective use of the system is necessary, but bringing branch level staff to headquarters is costly and time-consuming, and often needs to be scheduled on weekends. Using new communication technologies would reduce costs and save time.

Reality TV Program on Best Practices in Coffee Production in Timor-Leste

Elevating coffee culture

The challenge

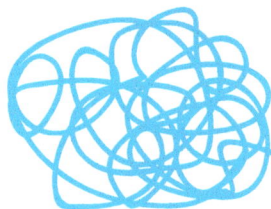

The innovation

Promoting better coffee and stimulating youth employment in Timor-Leste

Coffee plays an important role in Timor-Leste's economy. It is grown by almost one-third of all Timorese households and has been the country's largest non-oil export for the past 150 years, but there is still much room for improvement in terms of product quality and marketing.

ADB is supporting the industry to reach its full potential through a TA project amounting to $225,000 from ADB's Technical Assistance Special Fund to support the creation of a national development plan for the coffee sector.[5] Alongside this TA project, ADB was looking for an engaging and innovative way to promote the adoption of better coffee processing practices, and to disseminate information about good agricultural practices for coffee production, particularly with an eye to the requirements of specialty coffee markets. At the same time, stimulating youth participation in coffee farming and in agriculture more broadly in Timor-Leste is seen as a way to address both youth demand for employment and the needs of the coffee industry.

An "edutainment" reality television series

A series of five 20-minute "edutainment" reality television program episodes was created for broadcast on national television on best practices in coffee production over the growing and harvest seasons. With a budget of just $75,000, the locally produced series was filmed in Tetun. A lot of the innovation centered around how to get good results on a budget.

The show capitalized on an existing national coffee festival. It partnered with the local coffee association to identify four Dili baristas and four farmers from around the country, who were paired in teams and competed over the course of the series in various challenges, culminating in a barista competition at the festival using the coffee produced by the barista's farmer teammate. The show was broadcast on national TV in a prime slot, as well as through social media. Instructional videos were also made during the course of making the series.

---

5 ADB. 2016. *Technical Assistance to Timor-Leste for Support for Preparation of a National Coffee Sector Development Plan.* Manila. https://www.adb.org/projects/50334-001/main#project-overview

Learning point

What went well

Coffee production quality improved and the pilot accelerated the emergence of a group of young Timorese coffee entrepreneurs entering the coffee business. The winning team of farmer and barista have since gone into business together (Box 1). One of the episodes entailed a processing boot camp, which was held at a facility owned by a young Timorese entrepreneur. This prime example of young people returning to farming gained national exposure through the show, and a New Zealand specialty coffee company subsequently partnered with the owner. The show boosted the visibility of the Timor-Leste Coffee Association by giving it a more prominent role, reinforcing its place as a stakeholder in the development and implementation of the country's coffee sector development plan.

What could have been better

A budget big enough to also have a communications and social media campaign around the TV series would have really brought the project to life. With only one episode a month, it was insufficient to sustain interest, and the pilot needed more content across different media. The procurement times were also very time consuming relative to the small size of the budget, and more human resources for this, or simpler procurement processes, would have eased the way of the pilot significantly.

Box 1: From Farm to Bar, High Quality All the Way

In 2018, Fatima Moniz Suares had been a barista in Dili, Timor-Leste for 5 years, and she thought she knew coffee. While she was certainly highly knowledgeable about coffee beans and how to make a perfect brew, she had no idea how hard it was to be a coffee farmer. It was when she was invited to partner with coffee farmer Jorge Lopes as contestants on a reality TV show funded by the Asian Development Bank's Unlocking Innovation for Development technical assistance project that she saw firsthand the labor that goes into every sack of coffee beans.

"It was a really very interesting experience," she says. "The baristas didn't know the hard work of being a farmer, and the farmers didn't understand what the baristas were doing. So, we both had to work together to improve coffee quality."

The pilot added a lot to both the baristas' and the farmers' understanding. "Experts from Colombia came in and we were very happy to meet them. It was a great way for the Timorese to develop their coffee industry," says Suares.

The duo has since gone into business together, with Lopes' coffee beans in the grinder at Fatima Café in Dili, and on sale to customers to take home. "I hope my company will promote high-quality coffee in Timor-Leste," she says.

Source: Asian Development Bank.

WOMEN EMPOWERMENT

2.2
Dashboard on Child Marriage in Indonesia

Facing the facts about child marriage

The challenge

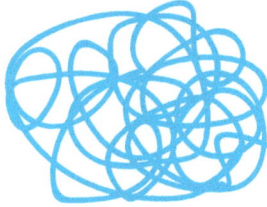

The innovation

Access to actionable data on child marriage in Indonesia

Not only is child marriage a human rights violation, it also deprives girls of their fundamental rights to health, education, and safety. In Indonesia, 14% of girls are married before the age of 18 years, and according to UNICEF, Indonesia has 1,459,000 child brides—the eighth highest absolute number in the world—and in East Java, both maternal mortality and early marriage rates are particularly high.[6] Provincial and district governments, religious leaders, and civil society have spoken out against child marriage and have committed to tackling it. Child marriage is as high as 30% in some districts in East Java, but local governments lack district-level data to better understand the drivers and services needed to address it in their constituencies, monitor progress toward eliminating child marriage, and support other local government efforts to meet the SDG 5.3 target of ending child marriages.

Local dashboards on child marriage

The pilot operated under the umbrella of an existing $1 million TA project aimed at strengthening government and civil society cooperation to improve public services. The existing Kinerja ADB project had fostered trust with both local government officials and community-based organizations. Districts have substantial decision-making authority and are responsible for providing some important health and education services following the country's decentralization reforms. The work under the Kinerja project showed that while participatory local policy dialogues have been strengthened through the project, they could be even more effective in identifying targeted and evidence-based interventions and appropriate policy responses when having access to local data. So far, effective compilation and use of data at district level was lacking and data were barely used for local decision-making purposes.

Under the pilot, ADB worked with government officials in selected districts of East Java to develop dashboards on child marriage by providing systematic and step-by-step capacity development training on indicator development, data mapping and collection, data visualization on dashboards, and analysis on child marriage and its associated drivers.[7] It was based on a well-established "Girls Not Brides" conceptual framework to tackle the drivers of child marriage, which had not been used before in Indonesia.

Data visualization on dashboards enables presentation of population data in an innovative way that is both content-rich and easy to understand. Dashboards were developed as tools to improve access to data and information by different stakeholder groups for various purposes, such as easy monitoring of progress toward ending child marriage, raising awareness on child marriage, designing targeted programs, and informing on the progress and efforts of government to tackle the drivers of child marriage to enhance accountability. The dashboards equip the various district offices that have a role in tackling child marriage with vital baseline data about the gaps, and better

---

[6] Girls Not Brides. Child Marriage Atlas: Indonesia. https://www.girlsnotbrides.org/where-does-it-happen/atlas/indonesia.
[7] ADB. 2016. *Regional Technical Assistance on Strengthening Government and Civil Society Cooperation and Civil Society Cooperation in Open Government Partnerships to Improve Public Services*. Manila.

understanding of how the services they provide should contribute toward ending child marriage.[8]

The 19 dashboards per district contributed to awareness raising, with strong leadership from the respective district heads and also involving a network of wives of government officials. It continues to contribute to more targeted and evidence-based interventions as well as informed decision-making and policy-making to tackle child marriage. The pilot took one development challenge—child marriage—and used it to demonstrate the utility of data dashboards to inform policy, measure progress toward development outcomes, including the SDGs, and improve accountability measures. The districts will develop standard operating procedures for updating the dashboards regularly. The district governments are now considering dashboard usage for other sectors, such as agriculture and fisheries, and have budgeted for the needed dashboard software in the next years' district budget. Further, training of trainers is planned for the dashboard development teams trained under the pilot for potential replication in other districts.

Child marriage is an issue that affects multiple sectors, and the pilot's capacity-building workshops brought people together for the first time from health, planning, religious affairs, education, and girl empowerment. Creating a dashboard was a very consultative process, giving participants the language and conceptual framework to have conversations with each other about a cross-sector issue to identify the indicators and related data they each need to take action. There was also a high degree of participant ownership. Participatory forums that have been established under the Kinerja project can use the dashboards to strengthen their local policy dialogues on improving services and achieving development outcomes. It can be used as a call to action on localizing the SDG agenda.

Learning point

What went well

The pilot shifted the mindset of government counterparts from collecting data to interpreting and using data for service delivery improvements and achieving development outcomes. The conceptual framework and indicators developed by ADB enabled presentation of data against identifiable targets. The project methodology enabled district officials from different sectors to take a consultative approach to reach a common understanding of drivers of child marriage, the services required to address it, and to better coordinate for more efficient service delivery and monitoring of activities and results.

Contrary to many conventional "data for development" and dashboard projects, the innovative approach was to do this at the lowest possible local government unit in a highly consultative and participatory manner. One of the biggest successes of this pilot was mapping and compiling data located in multiple government departments that had not previously been pulled together to get a more comprehensive picture of the drivers of child marriage in the respective districts. The conceptual indicator framework that was developed as a first step gave district officials more insights into the

[8] This includes the District Planning Office (Badan Perencana Pembangunan Daerah, BAPPEDA), the District Women's Empowerment Office, the District Health Office, the District Education Office, the District Social Affairs Office, and the Local Religious Affairs Office.

complex dynamics of child marriage and its drivers that they previously did not consider. Much of the data were previously paper-based and needed digitization. The cooperation between different local government departments was unprecedented. The stakeholders involved were truly appreciative about the participatory and systematic step-by-step process of developing the dashboards and the insights they gained on child marriage and how to tackle it along the way.

What could have been better

The project only had provision for a limited number of face-to-face training and mentoring sessions. More face-to-face sessions would have been more beneficial than off-site mentoring support. Staff trained on the Tableau software were more inclined to focus on the information technology part, but had limited capacity to understand the data part. Although the project's methodology required close collaboration between the dashboard developers and program managers and decision makers, this did not happen as much as was needed.

> "
> These dashboards have shown the condition of Lumajang District, and will help all government offices in Kab. Lumajang make the appropriate policy to suppress child marriage. The dashboard is one of facilities that uses information technology to support the better implementation of Kab. Lumajang programs, and it is in line with Lumajang's plan to be a Smart City. All government offices should welcome data related to the current condition, scheduling periodic updating, so it will be the reference for decision.
> "

Agus Triyono, Lumajang Local Secretary Assistant

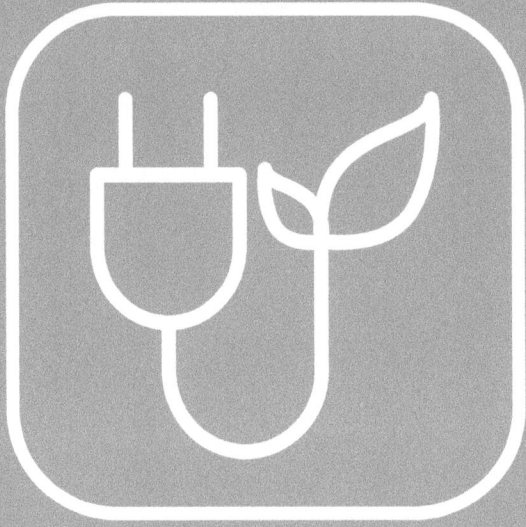

SUSTAINABLE ENERGY

2.7

An Innovative Utility Energy Services Model to Implement a Large-Scale Energy Efficiency Program in Thailand

Producing more with less energy

The challenge

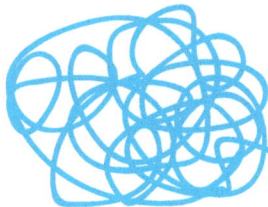

The innovation

Meeting ambitious targets for electricity savings across multiple sectors

The Government of Thailand aims to build a globally competitive green growth economy that reduces carbon emissions and creates well-paying, skilled employment opportunities that are not easily outsourced to other countries. To support this, it has set ambitious targets for electricity savings in three major economic sectors: residential, commercial and public services, and industry. Thailand's state-owned electricity distribution utility, the Provincial Electricity Authority (PEA), is well-positioned to be a leader in supporting Thailand's economy to produce more with less energy and enable consumers to reduce their cost of electricity consumption, but it will take an innovative private–public partnership approach to implement an energy savings program that is mutually beneficial to all stakeholder needs.

A utility energy services model that scales energy efficiency

Extensive research shows that the electricity generation and distribution utility sector is changing. Utilities are adapting their business model to new technologies and business processes. The PEA requested support from ADB in designing and implementing an innovative private–public partnership approach.

This TA component, which will start in early 2020 and run through mid-2020, will support the PEA with the design of a utility energy services model to scale the implementation of energy efficiency solutions in Thailand. The concept is that the PEA will leverage its existing relationship with customers (marketing, funding, billing) and manage the delivery of energy savings in residential, commercial and public buildings, and industrial complexes. At the same time, it will partner with third-party providers to enable efficient and focused service delivery (e.g., audits, sales, and installation management).

The objectives of the project are to design the utility energy services model, establish a financing mechanism for the PEA to raise capital for their energy efficiency offerings from ADB and other institutions, and prepare the pilot implementation of the energy-efficiency program, which will include identification of a small group of customers to test the core elements of the utility energy services model and refine the customer adoption strategy. The TA project will also determine the carbon emissions reduction and economic benefits that will be achieved with a large-scale and nationwide energy efficiency program.

RECOMMENDATIONS

Expand the internal innovation process and create a clear channel for innovative ideas to be shared, critiqued, and pitched for funding.

Establish an innovation hub to provide physical and virtual space, time, and resources for ADB staff to run selected projects through an innovation process, spanning identification of the problem or challenge, ideation, solutions, testing, evaluating, and planning for scale. The hub can also provide space to work collaboratively on a project, bring together diverse experts and offer training opportunities for ADB staff to apply innovation tools.

Create more flexible funding modalities so that innovative ideas are not suffocated by the procurement processes designed for large-scale, conventional projects. Not all innovation should be tied to loans or TA projects. This restriction may deter project officers from pitching for funding for new ideas without obvious TA or loan benefits. Moreover, the connections, goodwill, and experience gained in innovation pilots can feed into future loan and TA work, even if that is not clear at the outset.

Support the creation of project specific innovation teams, drawing together required expertise from across different departments within ADB and from outside the bank, to work with innovators to bring ideas to fruition.

Leverage ADB's unique position in the development community, its ability to connect with the public, private and third sectors, and its trusted partner status to convene diverse partners to design and implement innovations. Support projects that enable collaboration with other development agencies.

Incentivize the private sector to work on demonstration projects through preferential procurement terms for companies that share the risk on trying out innovative ideas, for example through innovation challenge prizes.

Develop innovative ideas that can be adopted by ADB or other agencies, based on the development case put forward as a result of the ADB-led innovation pilot or demonstration project.

Learn from failures and foster an environment where people can discuss failures openly. This requires deep knowledge of country, sector, and thematic contexts to ensure that failure is not happening because of poor performance.

Facilitate collaboration with other development agencies and support both direct ADB financing for innovative projects, and ADB piloting for projects, which are then adopted by others after testing by ADB.

Have a focal point for the different regions. What innovation looks like in the Pacific islands could be very different from what it looks like in South Asia, for example.

www.ingramcontent.com/pod-product-compliance
Lightning Source LLC
Chambersburg PA
CBHW061225270326
41927CB00025B/3499